Praise for *Radiant*

Diane Scharper describes unflinchingly how cancer causes the sky to fall in on our lives. With these poems she builds a roof, joist by joist and beam by beam, that gives us shelter from that falling.

> ✳Michael Collier
> Poet and Professor,
> University of Maryland
> Director,
> Breadloaf Writers' Conference

Diane Scharper gives a voice to the silent cries of a suffering heart and a ringing affirmation of love that cannot be extinguished. I doubt there is any adult human being who will not empathize, understand, and ultimately find comfort in this small volume of prayer/poems.

> ✳Ruthann Williams, OP
> Author, *Healing Your Grief*

Diane Scharper verily has 'the gift'—it glows in her ingenious feel for metaphor, her taut beauty, and her whipsnap endings.

> ✳Joseph Gallagher
> Retired Priest and Author,
> *To Hell and Back with Dante*

[These are] ...shimmering poems that do pirouettes around death.

These poems are very inviting...and prayers are always invitations, are always inviting.

Grief is not easy. Easy comfort is an oxymoron in a time of loss. Diane Scharper's collection comforts with its electric strangeness, its heart-starting jolt, its difficult beauty.

Scharper's prayer/poems are an eloquent expression of the journey through grief; I heard in them plaintive echoes of Job's heaven-hurled cries.

RADIANT

RADIANT

Prayer/Poems
by

Diane Scharper

Cathedral Foundation Press
Baltimore, Maryland

Printed and bound in the United States of America.

1 2 3 4 5   05 04 03 02 01 00 99 98 97 96

Library of Congress Cataloging-in-Publication Data
Scharper, Diane, 1942-
Radiant : prayer/poems / by Diane Scharper.
p.   cm.
ISBN 1-885938-23-3
1. Cancer--Patients--Poetry.   2. Religious poetry, American.
I. Title.
PS3569.C4745R33 1996
811'.54--dc20   96-13767
                                                                              CIP

Cathedral Foundation Press
P.O. Box 777
Baltimore, Maryland 21203

Publisher: Daniel L. Medinger
Editor: Gregg A. Wilhelm
Assistant Manager: Patti Medinger
Book design: Sue Seiler
Cover design: Steve Fabijanski
Author photo: Denise Walker

Cover art: Christ heals St. Peregrine, patron saint of cancer victims

*This book is dedicated
to the memory of
Frank Willard Waesche.*

Acknowledgments

I wish to thank my family
without whose help I could not
have written this book.
Thanks also to the gracious people
at Cathedral Foundation Press
for making the book possible.

What, do you wish to know your Lord's meaning in this thing? Know it well, love was his meaning. Who reveals it to you? Love. What did he reveal to you? Love. Why does he reveal it to you? For Love. Remain in this, and you will know more of the same.

Showings
Julian of Norwich
1342 c.-1423

$\mathcal{C}$ontents

Foreword

Grief is a persistent, gnawing, ever-present uninvited guest. Sometimes it takes a room in our being and stays a lifetime, coming and going, like a visitor with his own key. We might go days or even weeks without knowing grief and then collide in the hall in the dark of night.

Grief is personal. It's not the same for any of us. What might help you may not help me. Only those who have not experienced the deep wrenching pain of grief can insist that grief is orderly and numbered. Grief for me followed death, the death of my son. I suspect that grief moved in with Diane Scharper before the death of her father. Her grief probably began when her father was diagnosed with cancer. Cancer, the word the world has learned to dread. Cancer, the word that sent Diane Scharper's world spinning.

This collection of poems is the result of Ms. Scharper's journey of tears, journey of fears, journey of faith. They are prayers, these poems, for in her pain she turns to God. Initially, after the stunned spinning, she is filled with hope. Then she wrestles with hopelessness and once more knows hope. Finally, with the death of her father vanishing all hope, she unexpectedly finds hope in the smile on her dying father's face.

Her thoughts turn to theology. Why was her father smiling as he died? How could God allow his pain? Why would God make a world like this? What does it all mean? Does it mean anything at all? Why do we have to watch someone we love go through such pain? Why do we have to go through such an ordeal? How does the survivor who has worked so hard with the cancer patient deal with the pain when hope is gone? And back to that question: why was her father smiling?

The result of Ms. Scharper's prayer is a remarkable little volume of poetry that addresses the raw pain that she endured, the raw pain that so many of us in this world are asked to endure.

The amazing part is that Ms. Scharper takes the reader on a journey into her pain, but it is a gentle journey. She holds our hands in the hospital corridors. We see through her eyes both the horror and the heaven of "life" in the hospital. We feel her fear as she hears the diagnosis, hears medical terms that sound cold and impersonal, if not downright frightening. She screams the "No!" that we all feel when we get some very bad news, and yet, in her denial, she is reaching for hope for the life of this father she loves so very much.

She will not allow him to die, so she is frenzied in her search for wellness. She is "breathless" (the title of the first group of poems) with her plans for his survival. If they do everything right, God will not allow him to die. The reader feels the confusion, the chaos, the inability to think. We are in a strange land. There is a surrealistic feel to the hospital machinery, to the testing, to the sound of the doctors' voices. We have the overwhelming desire "to do something." There must be something to do to stop the avalanche of her father's illness. In her breathlessness, she longs for quiet. She prays, still breathless. We pray, too.

Just when the reader is filled with this breathlessness, Ms. Scharper changes the mood, for she knows only too well the unexplained moodiness of grief. Just when we have worked ourselves into a breathless frenzy, we are stilled. Just when we have been rallied to "do something," Ms. Scharper takes us to another room. She gives us a glimpse into what her father might have been feeling. We are allowed to stand in his hospital room and observe...if we are quiet and still. We stand by the window and watch his "spirit made flesh" (the title of the second section of poems). We watch and with Ms. Scharper, we pray. If we are still enough, we may get a glimpse into his soul...or is it the soul of Ms. Scharper? Wherever we are, we are still, and we pray.

The sufferer can take no more. We are exhausted with the frenzy, exhausted by the stillness of the deep speaking to deep. Ms. Scharper with her considerable poetic ability knows we need a change of pace. I had expected to be led into a beautiful forest. I had expected to sit by a stream and listen to the water follow where the stones would lead. Instead, without asking, she leads us to a room where we are forced to "wrestle the Angel of Death" (the third section). Her father has wrestled the Angel. Ms. Scharper has wrestled the Angel. The reader, too, wrestles, if briefly, all too aware that the bell tolls for all of us. We pray.

And it tolls for Ms. Scharper's father. In "Ghost" (the fourth section), she experiences the presence of the one who is no longer present. The days that follow death are almost unbearably beautiful. The one that you love—the one who left you and walked away with the Angel of Death—still lingers in the hallways of your heart. You see him in his favorite chair. You hear his voice as he enters the house. You wait for him to call. You see him in a passing car. You cry to him on a starry evening. You still feel the warmth of his body in his sweater. He has gone and, yet, he has not gone. It is all a big mistake because you just talked to him yesterday. You just held him. You just laughed together.

If nobody else knows it, God does...you and God. You pray.

In the final section, Ms. Scharper brings us to grief. Actually, she not so much brings us as she invites us. She's going there herself, and we are welcome to come along. One has the feeling that she is very comfortable with grief. She has made friends with grief. She has spent a lot of time there. She has gained from her questioning, from her prayers, but she allows the reader to grieve as the reader wants. She doesn't suggest that we must grieve the way she has grieved. She's not selling anything. She's sharing something. She has spent a great deal of time on the question of her father's smile. She's spent a great deal of time praying her poems. God has been with her, and she wants to tell us that. There is a reverence in her grief, for as she points out, grief is a part of God. God, the artist, "paints the canvas on which I found myself." We were created to love just as we were created to cry.

Diane Scharper found the blessedness of tears in her father's smiling benediction. Her poems are radiant. She has prayed. Thanks to her, we have all prayed.

Ann Weems
St. Louis, Missouri
March, 1996

Introduction

At 3:55 a.m., the phone on my mother's night table rang. My dad was in cardiac arrest. We dressed quickly and rushed to the hospital. Had the doctors resuscitated him? *Could* he be resuscitated? Or was it finally over? We did not know what to expect.

My dad was hospitalized the previous morning for *tic douloureux*, intense pain caused by trauma to the trigeminal nerve. In his case the trauma started with radiation treatment for head and neck cancer. As painful as it was, it seemed a small price to pay for thirteen cancer-free years. We realized that when his cancer recurred. This time the odds were harder to beat.

Yet my dad always looked on the bright side. He battled his cancer up to the end. Helping him, I learned about courage, love, and persistence.

But most of all, I learned to admire my dad. One of eight boys, my father grew up near Pimlico Race Track in Baltimore during the Depression. Later, he served in World War II and took part in the Normandy invasion. "Crawling over a beach with guns firing at you," he explained, "makes you or breaks you."

It obviously "made" him, because he seemed ready for anything. "Life's too short to give up," he said. By the end of the war, Dad had lost most of his thick red hair, but that didn't bother my mother.

Mom was a quiet woman who wondered what drove this man who worked hard, played hard, and liked a day off to go to the race track. Something about horse racing excited him. Maybe it was the competition. Maybe it was because he liked to go with the winner.

I was a mama's girl. One day Mom and Dad bought me a necklace. It was inscribed with the words, "My heart belongs to Daddy." No, I assured everyone, my heart belongs to Mom. As I grew up, I wrote poems, essays, and book reviews. When they were published, I clipped them and gave them to Mom, not Daddy. As I saw it, he wouldn't understand.

But when his cancer recurred after being in remission for thirteen years, I began to see another side to my father. A tumor grew on his tongue. The surgeon removed it and tied Daddy's tongue, making it difficult for him to speak and difficult for others to understand him.

How ironic that I, who had never been particularly close to my father, became close to him now.

I understood his halting speech. When he garbled his words, I "ungarbled" them. Sometimes, I even intuited his responses.

My Dad underwent several more operations during the next year or so. A cyst grew on his tongue; one grew on his tonsil; one even grew out of his neck. Dad, Mom, and I felt we should more aggressively fight the disease. So we asked for a second opinion. The surgeon directed us to chemotherapy.

Soon, we checked into the University of Maryland Cancer Center. Daddy brought pajamas, underwear, my cassette player, and a good attitude. He planned to listen to Glenn Miller (he loved to dance and enjoyed the big bands), take the medicine, and get well. When Mom and I left him that first day, he told me to get him a copy of *The Sun* paper. He wanted to catch up with the news.

I visited him everyday and began to read him sections from the various books that I was reviewing. Once in a while, we talked about a book and tried to determine the author's point. When my reviews were printed, I gave them to him. He made comments about them. Gradually, I found myself thinking of him as an audience. And he had a good effect on my writing. I found myself trying to be clearer and more direct.

Then one night, Daddy ran a high fever. I was

already home when I learned that he developed pneumonia in both lungs. When the doctor called to tell me how Daddy was doing, I pictured Death coming to my dad's room and his doctor locking the door.

She explained that she had given Daddy high-powered antibiotics and planned to increase his oxygen. "He's iffy," she said, "iffy at best."

Tears rushed up into my eyes, and I quickly got off the phone; I did not want her to hear me cry. "Take care," she told me. It was too late to drive back to the hospital, so I prayed and tried to write a book review.

If writing possesses a magic power, I wanted to summon it then. I wrote and thought of Daddy, sent him love and healing thoughts. Those thoughts were the genesis of these prayer/poems. I wanted to write poems for him then, but couldn't gather the necessary distance from my subject. It would be several years before I wrote these poems. At that time, I had only a few words.

If you fall, I told him in a series of silent messages, *we'll catch you. Your doctor and I will catch you. If you fall, Daddy*, I thought, *fall deeply into love. Take care.*

We won that battle, but the war was far from over. Daddy's body weakened, and the cancer grew immune to the current combination of drugs.

So, we found a new doctor and a new chemotherapy. Things got worse. I knew it, but Daddy didn't, and he courageously fought on.

One day a cancer survivor visited him, and Daddy announced that he, too, was in remission. "How do you know?" Mom asked. He explained that he just knew. His body told him, and he knew. That was my dad—always ready to hope and work for the best.

But x-rays showed that his tumor had grown. It pushed the food down the wrong pipe. He could not swallow. One of his doctors suggested a stomach peg. Daddy's eyes narrowed. "It's no big deal," I told him. "You can eat through a plastic tube in your stomach."

How, I wondered, could I dare say that this was "no big deal"? How could I call this "eating"? It doesn't have to be permanent, I reassured him. Besides, another medicine was added to the mix. With any luck, the tumor would shrink. And he'd be able to eat by mouth again.

Even if it didn't look like it, I said, we were on the upswing. And he didn't have to stay in the hospital. "Just come once a week. We'll make it," I almost convinced myself.

We worked at it for a month. Daddy came home; he was weak, but he got around with a walker. In no time, I told him, he'd be using a cane.

He agreed and planned to go to the races, when he felt stronger. Meanwhile, my daughter celebrated a birthday and received her first camera for a present. She took my dad's picture.

Soon Daddy gained a few pounds. He thought his weight would be back to normal in four or five months. One day while we were waiting to be seen at the hospital, the sun streamed brightly through the window. It bathed us in light, made us radiant, made us feel like dancing. I hugged him.

When the photographs came back from the developer, I studied my dad's picture. His skin seemed papery thin and gray. I looked at his neck and noticed that the tumor had grown even larger. *Don't say anything*, I decided.

Don't tell anyone, even his doctors, I thought, hiding the picture, as if doing that would make him better. My worst fear was that one of his doctors would tell him that he had no hope. I knew that one always had hope.

I was literally a walking example of that hope. I had polio when I was ten years old. The doctors told my parents that I would never walk again. But the doctors were wrong. After a year or so, I was able to walk and run as well as anyone else. My parents had prayed and thought that I was cured by prayers. I didn't know why I was able to walk. I only knew that there is always room for hope, and that doctors, with all their knowledge and skill, don't know everything. I also knew that Daddy needed to look at the bright side, as he always did.

Then the *tic douloureux* started up with a vengeance. The pain was so severe that we rushed Daddy to the nearest hospital. The doctors planned to adjust his pain medicine and told us that he'd only be hospitalized for a day or so.

They gave him some morphine, and when he was settled in his room, his spirits rose. He read the race results. He asked me to set the phone up close to his bed. Around eight o'clock, he told us he was tired. "Played out," he said.

Early the next morning, the call came from the hospital. We went to him and saw that the struggle was over. The nurses explained that they had come to take his vital signs. His pressure was fine; his pulse was slow; then his heart skipped a beat, and another one, and another one, and he died. But, the nurses said, he died peacefully, with a smile on his face.

I looked at my dad, touched him. His head was already cold. His eyes were closed, but, yes, there was a smile on his lips. What, I wondered, could possibly make him smile? He must have realized that this was the end. Why did he look so satisfied? Did he see a tunnel of light? Did he see God? Did he see nothing?

"Is death the big nothing?" I asked myself. I felt cheated. He and I worked so hard at living. He didn't deserve to die. He deserved a gold medal, a Purple Heart, another heart beat. He deserved some say in this matter of his life, but he got nothing.

I was angry with everyone, including God. I could not pray. I could hardly write, although a book review was due a few days after my dad's death. I managed to get an extension from my editor and wondered why my dad couldn't get an extension on his life.

Gradually, I became less blocked, partly because time passed and partly because my editor was assigning books about death and dying. These helped me think through my father's death, while giving me a vehicle to express some of my own feelings. Soon I even managed to pray and to write a few poems about my dad, although I avoided looking too deeply into this corner of my psyche.

Several years passed before I was given the assignment to review *Lost & Found: A Journey Through Grief*, a memoir by Ellen Uzelac, a former reporter for *The Sun*. In the book, Ms. Uzelac describes her husband's battle with cancer in words that spoke directly to my heart.

She recalls the day her husband passed out in

his office and was wheeled across Calvert Street to Mercy Medical Center. They sat in a waiting room staring at nothing, hearing that dreaded word, tumor.

God, the power of that word. The Uzelacs felt unable to breathe, as if the whole world caved in around them. And in a way, it had. The book captured it all: the roller coaster of good news, bad news, hope, hopelessness, and uncertainty that make up the disease called "cancer."

Coincidentally, I had been visiting a friend at Mercy Medical Center, when my editor assigned me the Uzelac book. Mercy was also the hospital where my father's cancer was first diagnosed. I, too, felt as though the air had been knocked out of me. I, too, heard words about tumors and malignancies. I, too, felt weightless, my head spinning under the power of a word. Cancer.

The diagnosis creates a breathless rush of frenzied energy, similar to the children's story where the acorn falls from the tree, and Chicken Little rushes panic-stricken, warning his friends that the sky is falling.

With cancer, though, the sky really does fall. Ms. Uzelac and her husband were galvanized with energy. I could feel their energy as I read. My eyes were glued to the book. I read her words as if they contained the secret of life.

Yet, when it came time to write the review, I didn't know what approach to take. If I wrote what I felt, my heart would break. My dad bravely battled cancer. I took him for treatments, check ups. I visited him in the hospital. We became partners.

How could I put into words the memories that the book called up in me? I would blab my feelings, like tears, all over the page. So I opted for restraint. I put only a few sentences about my dad into the review, ending my comments by saying that I was examining the contents of my heart. God, was I ever.

I continued that examination for the next several weeks. Everything I did seemed to evoke the memories I had of that painful time with my dad. My feelings surged forward. I began writing my own memoir in the form of poems.

I put everything that I had purposely left out of my book review into the poems. They, in turn, wrapped words around my feelings. I wrote poems remembering my father and the trips we made to the hospital. I could almost see the soft beige light of the waiting room, the stained glass reflection of the chapel, the votive candles, the hospital halls, every place we ventured on this journey.

If I wasn't writing the poems, I was thinking them. In a sense, the poems were thinking me. It was almost as if I could hear a voice telling me each poem. Was it God? I don't know to whom the voice belonged. The speaker isn't the point, though.

The point is that the voice carried me away. It spoke insistently and constantly. If I were quiet for a moment or so, I could hear a voice speaking from the back of my mind. At times, the voice seemed fearful. But it didn't give in to fear. It held emotion in check, preferring instead a note of wry humor.

When I write, I usually rewrite. But these poems were different. They came quickly and fairly easily. Some needed a little work. Some needed more intense revision. But in a miraculously short time, all were written.

The poems multiplied like the loaves and the fishes in the Bible story. I'd write a poem. Several days later, the poem broke open like two halves of a loaf, each half becoming a whole. Then I'd have two poems, which would sometimes break apart again yielding more poems.

I seemed to be poetry's instrument, in what felt to be a deeply religious experience. God and I were talking. These poems are what we said. In that sense, these poems are prayers, the collection being one long prayer.

People who are sick sometimes have intense religious experiences. Writer Reynolds Price, for example, believed that he saw Christ who healed him from his cancer. I wasn't sick, but I grew close to my father during his illness. Now five years later, I was writing poems about him.

As I wrote them, I felt caught up in something I can only describe as God. "What the Angel Said," one of these poems, puts it this way: "You are the words. He (God) is this poem." I could see that God needs us as the poem needs words. In a sense, we are God's medium. Simultaneously, we need God; words without the poem are empty, because the poem is the spirit (in this case, Holy Spirit) that gives rise to the words.

I call the words "Prayer/Poems," partly because these poems began as prayers for my father and partly because these poems go on a spiritual quest. I wrote them trying to figure out the meaning of my father's death.

We prayed. We did all the right things. Yet, my dad died. Why? I wanted to know. Why did God who loves us let this happen? Christ performed miracles all the time. Why didn't he perform one for us?

Blessed Julian of Norwich tried to answer a similar question. Julian, an anchoress, who lived in solitude in England, became deathly ill when she was thirty years old. She wondered why God would allow this to happen. Later, she saw the crucified Christ and experienced a series of visions. Those visions showed her that "love was his meaning."

Love is also my theme. As my dad and I battled his cancer, we grew closer to each other and to God. I hope readers will also feel that closeness in these poems.

Both poetry and theology look at our relationship with God. Theology looks more from God's perspective. Seeing God's power, for instance, theologians tell us to obey God's commandments. Poetry, though, looks from our perspective. Poets muse on people's need for love; they use words to recreate some of the emotions of love. And they call God "Love."

Many parts of the Mass use poetry. The Eucharist is a good example. Christ used words to create His Presence. We use the same words to recreate the Presence of One who is considered the Word of God.

Just as religious rituals often began as poetry, poetry often began as religion. The poet contemplates and searches for inspiration or is bestowed inspiration. "Inspired" means "breathed into." Interestingly, God created man by breathing into a handful of earth.

Prayer/poetry or sacred poetry has a long history. In fact, some of the earliest poems were prayers. One of the central texts of the Hindu religion, *The Upanishads*, is a prayer/poem, written in the eighth century B.C. Much of the Bible is sacred poetry (especially the Old Testament) and dates back several centuries B.C. In the New Testament, the Gospel of John begins by establishing reverence for the word: "In the beginning was the Word, and the Word was with God, and the Word was God."

Chinese and Japanese mystics wrote sacred poems. So did European poet/mystics (Hildegarde of Bingen, St. Francis of Assisi, Mechtilde of Magdeburg, Julian of Norwich, Dante, George Herbert, William Blake). More recently, there are T.S. Eliot, William Butler Yeats, and Gerard Manley Hopkins.

Many contemporary poets also write sacred poetry. Some of the better known ones include Thomas Merton, Daniel Berrigan, Pope John Paul II, and Louise Glück, who won the 1993 Pulitzer Prize for her book of poems, *The Wild Iris*.

Poetry and religion are two sides of the same coin. That coin ultimately belongs to God (not to Caesar) since poetry and religion connect us to the transcendent. Religion without poetry tends to shrivel up, becoming all text and no spirit. Unfortunately, the current age has abandoned much of the poetic character of religious rituals. I hope my poems can help restore part of that loss.

The book has five sections. The first section, "Breathless," describes my reactions (fear, denial, breathlessness, attempts to cope, to center, to pray) when my father's cancer recurred.

The second section, "Spirit Made Flesh," contains my prayers for my father and what I imagined to be his prayers. It tries to put into words what nature and God say to someone with a life-threatening illness and, more importantly, what the individual says in return.

The third section, "Wrestling The Angel," shifts the focus onto death (the angel of death/God). It is probably the most metaphysical section of the book. The poems describe my attempts to keep death away from my dad, which in a way was keeping it away from myself. It contains my doubts. It also contains my realization that God was with us, helping us to find ourselves and create ourselves through this ordeal, which I express in the prayer/poem "Ecce Homo."

"Ghost," the fourth section, describes my gradual realization that death is a benevolence. My father suffered terribly; death released him from that suffering. He accepted his death with a smile. I had to learn to embrace that death, and I did. These are the warmest poems in the collection. Their point is that love never ends, because all love is a part of

God.

"Elegy," the final section, shows how I've healed over time. These poems talk about, in a sense talk to, grief. Grief is almost personified here. When my dad died, grief came to take his place.

Grief, as I see it, is also part of God. How could it be anything else, since we grieve because we have lost someone we love? This section also refers back to the concept of God as "artist" who painted the canvas on which I found myself.

Finally, I've titled the book *Radiant*. "Radiant" plays on the word for cancer treatment, radiation being the healing waves of energy emitted by radioactive particles. "Radiant" is also the word for that inexpressibly beautiful quality of sunlight that sustains life on earth. I hope the poems are worthy of such a title.

BREATHLESS

Diagnosis

While the doctor describes what looks like

a shadow in a black and white photograph,

you look at the opposite wall trying to find

a dark moon circling

an undiscovered planet.

Your father's eyes, meanwhile, have grown

larger and larger.

What big eyes he has.

"Hey blue eyes," you call out,

saying

nothing.

The Sickness

Wearing a space suit
and something
resembling a fishbowl,
your father is
floating away from you.
He has become an astronaut suspended
outside
the gleaming spaceship
of this hospital.
He's between earth and heaven
holding on,
while his legs fly out,

going someplace else.

Dealing With It

You are in a balloon

looking down at yellow sand

glistening under a bright sun.

Westerly winds make it nearly impossible

to hear exactly what is being said.

Only the sounds of sentences that make no sense

come.

Spacing Out

Better to make a poem

here

between the green tree tops

and

the blue sky.

You meet the sky's gaze.

How touching the sky is.

How it touches softly.

You do not touch your father.

You think of the trees.

Their effusive greens

touch like broccoli flowerets.

Would you like to ride in my

beautiful balloon?

You are here.

He is there.

Saying It

You see your father floating
by the unidentified flying object
that should be you
but probably isn't.
He looks like one of those pictures
of the earth rising, those space shots
caped in mist so touching, they take
your breath away. Reaching out from
your balloon, you say to him,
come aboard.

Masses

The doctor is speaking:
Masses.

We don't know whether
they're malignant
or not.

Masses,
she says in a low voice as
if she were praying.
How many prayers in a
mass?

Jesus, Jesus, Jesus
is a prayer.
You don't say it so much
as breathe it.

You don't breathe it so
much as let it cover you,
like clothes,

like brand new clothes.

Coping

Taking your father's hand,

you ask:

How do you like this new hat I am wearing?
And the gloves and the shoes?

This dress is blue-midnight blue,

like antique glass.

There is a moon at the center. It is covered with

stars.

Shall we dance?

Auld Lang Syne

At the farthest reach of the universe,

      you begin to pray.

Gray smoke appears

      then white.

Incense.
You wonder whether death
is
the
point
of everything.
No. No.
No, you are not meant for this,
although you know precisely
and more clearly than anything
you've ever known
that you are.

Bye

Where are we? you ask your father,
both of us having just fallen into
the black hole of the universe.

Where are we going? you ask.

Your father leaves you with strangers.
He leaves,
and you're sitting there
in the hospital waiting room,

      calling

          out to him.

Take Comfort

Everyone is talking. They put their words
on you like
yellow stick 'em notes.
Smiley faces.
You take them off. What do they say?
You listen, trying to connect
with this conversation.
Taking a large ball of string, you begin making
a hammock.
>Here,
>here,
>you say, tying knots.
Let us make a large net
and hold it carefully under him.

Alone

Standing on a balcony

   with a storm

      coming up and winds blowing clockwise

   and counter clockwise at least a hundred

miles an hour, you ask for

quiet.

Breathless

I.

X-Ray.
Amid
these smiling faces,
the white-skinned moon
bruises
easily.

II.

Mantra,
what keeps
the three of us going?
I ask.

"Ask again,"
says the light
flashing
among the leaves.

III.

Look at him
all arms and legs
—praying mantis—
        bug-eyed.

IV.

Falling

            I'm
                Not.

Spirit Made Flesh

Chapel

What's

going on

in here?, you ask.

This cancer's gonna get you.

He's a giant leech. He approaches

you smiling. Smack. Suck.

He's on your heart.

You listen

but can't hear

anything.

Spirit

Taking your father to the chapel,
you pray:

> Shake your tambourine now,
>
> doe-eyed Jewish boy.
>
> Shake it bending your head.

Over blades of grass is the wind-blown
sunlight,
and the storms.

Spirit Entering

Jesus,
may he have music,
you pray.
May melody,
a million times,
silver down
like stars.

Oh God, you say.
Oh God, you hear
to the tune of a song
someone (who sounds just like you)
is singing on the radio.

A Respite

Most kind and courteous God

whose voice does not speak in the

splashing rain,

whose feet do not walk

on the still surface of the lake,

let him drift on You like air

losing himself

until nothing is left.

A Few Questions

You leave a message
on his answering machine.
"I'm sending you healing thoughts
and prayer."
It is prayer in the shape of a poem.
What is prayer if it is not asking
that he become these words?
What is prayer if it is not asking
that he become?
What is prayer if it is not asking?
What is prayer if it is not?

What is prayer?

What is?

What?

Moment of Silence

What
is
prayer
if
it
is
not
asking
that
he
become
these
words,
caught
up
in
themselves,
lifted
darkly
on
their
soft
wings?

Life Asks Him

Am I the reflection in the lake that looks
down?

The fine hairs of the wildflower that float
away?

The gauzy seed parachuting off?

No,

he answers,

I am.

Nature Speaks to Him

Last night's dew is rising like breath smoke;

the air under the pine tree's
arch is turning to rain.

Come closer. As I talk, these woods stain you

with their darkness.
A million green eyes watch.

God Speaks to Him

I.

In the first dream,
the old man explains
that the door to this cave
is actually a bottomless illusion
made by the branches of trees, spreading
as far as the eye can see and farther. What he
doesn't explain is how much farther.
Your father, being too much
of a gentleman, doesn't ask
any questions, but tells
you about this
later.

II.

In the second dream,
        the old man explains that
                his wildest desire will be
                        fulfilled here at this door
                which opens very gradually
        and never closes. Does the
"his" refer to me, your father
wonders.

III.

In the third dream,
        your father speaks
                to the old man saying,
                        "You are the darkness
                        that I am drawn towards."
                It is more a question than
        a statement. The old man
says nothing.

Radiant

"Bright light shimmering,

I am flamed forth by you

becoming brilliant, pristine,

prismatic words made

from light—the brightest one

...being...

being

me."

The Waiting Room

Meanwhile,
your job is to count the tiny glass stones
in a kaleidoscope.

You arrange them
      (turn this to see
      stripes of sunshine
      and stars)
placing them to catch
the early morning breeze.
You call this waiting, "prayer."

You call anything "prayer."

Spirit Made Flesh

I.

Resting
on the thick white
silence,

you listen

II.

to it.

III.

A few
larger birds,
two or three
sparrows,
and a small
gray-breasted
nameless one, whom you would call
if you could,
swoop
from the trees

while singing.

IV.

Everything moves
in these branches

the brown leaves,
the winter buds redden.

V.

Hard-pressed
against
this rock
and nothing,

you alone

are still.

VI.

You think.

WRESTLING

THE

ANGEL

The Angel

Code 99.

Doctor Blue.

"Trouble," says the kindly old nun beside you.
A somewhat nervous receptionist explains
that each hospital has its own name for this
rushing, this fierce darkness that leaves him
breathless.

Angel of Death

Running from you, I think how easy it would be to mistake your wings for the sleeves of an over-sized sweater, how one could think your massive shoulders were a baggy coat. How easy to fall into your arms, bury my face on the soft wool of your garment. Knowing that you would speak to me, I say goodbye.

Ecce Homo

What is this yellow light entering through the window? I see you in my mind's eye. You are not you but a painting. You are the brush strokes or the hand holding the brush. You are the moment before the brush is placed when the eye decides where.

Doubts #1

God

(at least you think it's God)

is speaking in the first person, present tense:
Seeing clouds of gray dust, you give me a
name.

Hearing silence, you say I speak.
But it is you who speaks.
You are in love with love.

No matter how tenderly I might feel towards
you; we are left with the fact that you have
taken on death and that I can do nothing.

Doubts #2

I am sound without shape,
the bell's green echo winding through the
woods. My footprints follow the stream's
zigzag path and disappear among the leaves.

You only imagine my hands finger-combing
your hair; my eyes, soft and misted; my words
smiling.

Doubts #3

Here in this sanctuary,
beside the rows of flickering candle light,
you can see me
for what I am:

heat rising
on yellow wings,
your yellow wings.

Wrestling the Angel

I.

Crawling
over the ice,
his knees sink
a foot
or so.

II.

His bare hands
scooping snow
away from the blue spruce,

the
frozen
branches,

III.

re
lease him.

IV.

If
You
had a heart,
God,
It would break,

V.

re
membering.

GHOST

Secret

Going down this hall and down that,

outracing the pink phone notes being handed

to me, I call you my secret. I am aware of you

only when you begin speaking, which is right

now and always. Turning my face right and

left, I turn away and back. No one besides me

knows why I smell perfume whenever I think

of you.

Love Goes On and On

The minute I slow down, you catch up,
bringing the scent of invisible flowers.
Who are you
that I must think of you continuously,
looking for signs,
turning things over,
counting flower petals?
Just who are you?, I'm screaming.
You are
—I hear this said in a low voice—
barely a whisper:

(You are redder than roses.)

Jesus.

What the Angel Said

You are two parallel lines
lengthened infinitely.

You are the cloud's white.

You are what you can see
and what you cannot see.

You are the bow from which is sent the arrow
of morning.

You are the words.

He is this poem, this terse message spoken,
the cool rain making star marks on your hair.

The Long Haul

I've almost come to the end of this, knowing

it's not the end. I haven't avoided death but

have told myself that I have. With my father's

tear-stained smell on me, I'm wondering where

I go from here and what words can buy.

Ghost

I.

Trudging
through,

waist-high,
hip-high,

losing yourself,

II.

your
mind
is
not
on this,

III.

but
your heart is.

IV.

Tears

make

you

lighter.

V.

Afterwards,
alone,
under a blue sky
and a brilliant yellow sun,
in the waist-high drifts,

he
is
snow.

VI.

Nearly.

A Final Glimpse

It can be anything from the moon seen through
the leaves of the tree to the white cat climbing
up over the fence; even dust motes rising and
falling in the sunlight can tease down sweet
blue nothings. Being found after having been
long gone makes light pour through.

But catching a final glimpse of its silken hem,
wondering when it will return, and if it will,
      can
            bring
                  tears
                        to a
                              stone.

Grief

I.

At first I saw its mirage-like shimmer as heat
on the black macadam.

Only later did it become steam–his ghost
rising up from the hot street. Filling the space
he left behind was silence.

II.

Once in a while I noticed objects, such as the
white bark of the birch tree, or the moon's face
behind the clouds. Sometimes I could see rain
flatten out like a clover leaf against the
windshield, though whole shades of meaning
would pass me by.

It wasn't the little things I missed. It was every
thing. After the loneliness settled on me, I
could barely lift it off.

III.

Finding little comfort, I watched You take one
of the larger, one of the finer brushes.
Applying a gray wash,

You let Your thoughts ribbon down this way
and that trying to reach me over the rain.

IV.

After his death, You worked in water colors
and pencil sketches, drawing bird wings,
beady eyes, in the pine tree a half smile, the
rain's wistfulness. It was something like
Japanese calligraphy.

We knew this much that You would do any-
thing for me to keep the Green spell from
breaking.

V.

Green, Not Just Green, But Yellow Green,
Gray Green, Bright Chartreuse And White,
Pencil Shading, Brush Stroke, Straight Line,
Right Angle Mist,
Losing one's self in the mist.

Elegy

I.

Moving
Quickly
The cricket's last chirp

I look for it where it was.

II.

Rain
Soaked
Grass

You
Listen
For the green.

III.

Both of us
Watching

The tree's red color goes away.

IV.

Cloud
Crossing
The moon

Do you see it, too?

V.

White
Sweater
Caught
On the wood fence
You close the gate

VI.

It isn't you

The shining lights are only water on the street.

VII.

Wet leaves
Sticking
To my shoes

Someone
Thinks
Of you.

VIII.

Nobody
Here

Yellow rooms
Grow
Larger

IX.

Saying goodbye

Rain drops and the sound of rain
Collapse into each other.

X.

Gray
Moth
Flitting
At the window

Is that you?

Afterword

Over the past thirty-one years, I have learned to imagine the priestly ministry as being a companion to those on the journey through life.

I have been blessed to accompany pilgrims through the deserts of addictions to chemicals, through AIDS, through fractured and diminished self-esteem caused by poverty and oppression, through loss of loved ones by deaths natural and violent, and through terminal illness.

The journey through life is often difficult. It is always too short.

My experiences are rich and deep, but I never had the images and words to adequately speak the mystery of suffering and God's love for us as we grieve. Diane Scharper's *Radiant*, however, shines brightly with those words and images.

Her prayer/poems have been helpful to me in giving flesh to my experiences, and in understanding better what my eyes have seen and my ears have heard. They will be useful and powerful to all ministers, all pilgrims, all who have learned the lesson that there is no way out of a desert except through it, and that the journey itself is pregnant with God.

Thank you, Diane, for inviting us to journey with you. I understand myself and my fellow pilgrims a little bit better.

Rev. Samuel J. Lupico
Baltimore, Maryland
March, 1996

About the Author

A member of the Academy of American Poets and Delta Epsilon Sigma, Diane Scharper writes about poets and poetry for the *Baltimore Sun*. She reviews books for *The Catholic Review*, *City Paper*, *Maryland Poetry Review*, and the *Virginian Pilot*. A widely-published poet, Ms. Scharper lectures on modern poetry for the National Endowment for the Humanities. She graduated from the Johns Hopkins Writing Seminars and has been an adjunct professor of writing at Towson State University since 1986. Her first collection of poetry, *The Laughing Ladies*, was published in 1993.